BUSINESS ENGLISH

AN INDIVIDUALISED LEARNING PROGRAMME

Teachers' Manual

PETER WILBERG   MICHAEL LEWIS

D1585565

Language Teaching Publications
35 Church Road Hove BN3 2BE

ISBN   Bound edition   0 906717 72 8
        Looseleaf edition   0 906717 79 5
        Teachers' Manual   0 906717 80 9

Printed in England by Commercial Colour Press, London E7.

Business English is based on an idea by Peter Wilberg. The materials have been developed
by Peter Wilberg and Michael Lewis. The cross-cultural material was contributed by Philip
O'Connor of Language Training Services in consultation with Michael Lewis.

CONTENTS

1. INTRODUCTION

BUSINESS ENGLISH COURSES

The term "business English" covers many different kinds of courses. There are pre-service courses which are usually quite extensive, and where the participants have little or no actual business experience. These contrast in many ways from courses provided for business people already at work. These latter tend to be either in-company, intensive courses, or courses of relatively short duration in private language schools.

It is immediately apparent that the materials and course design requirements of pre-service and in-service courses are, or should be, vastly different. All too often, however, lack of appropriate material has resulted in the same or similar materials being used on the two courses.

The very term "business English" provokes debate. Some people believe that "business English" is little more than general English in a business context; others believe that much more student-specific materials can be devised, and that business English courses will involve a large element of job-specific vocabulary work. There is, of course, truth in each of these arguments, and this leads to one of the central ideas which underlies all business courses – the need for compromise. The compromises are of several kinds:

between general and specific language

between job-specific, company-specific, and subject-specific language

between effective, but defective communication and grammatical accuracy

These points, however, cover only the compromises related to the language which is taught. A number of other important compromises are frequently part of such courses:

The client's requirements versus the student's requirements

Many in-service business English courses are provided for employees by their employers. The client, who is paying for the course, is most frequently a company. The language courses provided for its employees almost certainly form part of a more complex system of company courses. The company will impose requirements about course timing, length and content, and (much more questionably) even course success rates. Those who are providing such courses cannot afford to ignore such client requirements. These, however, may differ sharply from the requirements of the individual student who comes on such a course. The student may be learning English for quite different purposes to those perceived by his or her employer; may be contemplating a job change, or have other interests unknown to the employer. A course will only be "successful" if it can, somehow, satisfy both client and student, even when these needs are in conflict.

Wants versus needs

Either the client or the student must state very clearly what they want from an in-service course. As schools are only too well aware, however, the student's actual language needs may differ wildly from what is requested, by either client or student. The student's general language level may be much lower than either the student or employer is prepared to admit. Alternatively, the desired areas of improvement may be based on a very naive view of language learning so that, requests such as "I need to improve my vocabulary", while superficially a clearly stated objective, may not at all be the most efficient way for students to improve their communicative effectiveness.

Needs versus possibilities

Many in-service courses are preceded (either before the course begins, or on day one of the course) by some form of needs analysis. Although these differ in form, extent and effectiveness, they will often suggest that the student needs, for example, 90 hours tuition to achieve certain stated objectives. In practice, either student or client may then announce that only 30 hours spread over two weeks, or a one week high intensity course is possible. Yet again, schools which want to stay in business have to accept these constraints and reach some sort of compromise between the student's declared needs and objectives, and what is possible with the time and resources available.

Everyone involved in the provision of business English courses will be only too aware of the above constraints. Many will be able to add fairly easily to the list of factors which result in all business courses being compromises between, or among, many conflicting demands. **Business English** can certainly not resolve all of these compromises but it has been designed with these problems in mind. It is a great deal more flexible and adaptable than any conventional business English course.

TRADITIONAL SOLUTIONS

There seem to be two conventional approaches to the provision of business English courses. One is what we may call the "course book approach". This involves giving the student a basic text book which closely resembles a general English course. It tends to be a fairly large book, arranged in units, where each unit follows a standard pattern such as presentation text or dialogue, comprehension questions, vocabulary and grammar work, discussion etc.

The advantages of such course books are clear – they provide a clear **sequence** of work, a **balance** of different kinds of language activity, and allow student, teacher and institution to "know where we are".

It seems to us that such an approach has much to commend it for pre-service courses, where, as we have said, students frequently have little on-the-job experience, and the courses are, of their nature, rather general and quite extensive in time. The advantage of a conventional course book in such circumstances is clear.

What we are much less happy about is the use of such conventional course books for in-service courses. Many organisers of such courses will be fully aware of the compromise they make when they advertise or promote their schools to a company as providing "tailor-made" courses, only, after doing a needs analysis to decide that the student's needs will be perfectly fulfilled by the use of a standard text book! This may be an institutional convenience, or even necessity but it is perhaps the clearest example of the compromises used in constructing such courses!

The second approach may be characterised as "the photo-copy approach". Here, the student is provided with a file, to which during the course are added an endless string of photocopies taken from business English course books, the Financial Times, professional journals, exercises from grammar books etc. This approach tends to be favoured by many schools providing in-service courses, and, again its appeal is obvious – it is possible to choose materials which are (more or less) relevant to the student's declared objectives, and to tailor course content to a greater or lesser extent to job-specific needs.

Unfortunately, this approach has serious disadvantages. Much of the photocopied material is illegally copied; there is no overall course plan available to student or teacher; finding generally suitable materials is more difficult than it seems and, finally but less obviously, the course content is still largely dictated by the teacher rather than the student.

A RADICAL NEW APPROACH

Business English represents a radical new approach to the provision of in-service business English courses. It represents a third alternative, being neither a conventional course book, nor requiring extensive photocopying. It is based on two radically new, and sharply different, principles. These are:

a. The content of an in-service business English course should, as far as possible, be provided by the **student**. In general, the **language** is provided by the **teacher**, but the **content** is provided by the **student**. The detailed working out of this idea is discussed extensively below.

b. The object with which the student is working – the book – should be designed from the perspective of a business person, not that of the language teacher. This principle requires some explanation.

In the past, business English courses, whether based on a course book or photo-copies, have not given the student an accurate, complete, and re-accessible record of the material studied during the course. Everyone is familiar with the idea of students underlining unknown words in texts, writing in the margins, and possibly keeping a vocabulary book. All of this, while common in general English language teaching, is very far from ideal for **any** student, certainly not for the professional doing a high quality (and frequently highly priced) business English course. There is little point in the student studying language, and then recording it, unless that material can be **re-accessed, revised**, and **used** after the course, as occasion demands. Marginal notes on photocopies, and a traditional vocabulary book, will not provide this permanent re-usable record.

Many business students are very used to recording information they need in prepared formats to allow the organisation and re-accession of the information in a variety of ways. Many of these students will not use a small diary, but will be very familiar with a "personal organiser", in which different sections record information of different kinds, and the formats of the pages help you to record the information in effective and re-accessible ways.

Business English has been designed with these ideas in mind. It is arranged in sections, the pages provide a range of formats which allow the organisation and re-accessing of information, and the page format itself, in which the word 'Organiser' occurs as part of the page format for every page, helps to remind the student that they are not simply recording what they learn, but **organising the information so that they can re-access the information when it is needed.**

One of the main innovations of **Business English** is the provision of sophisticated recording formats likely to be useful to, and appeal to, the student used to the sophisticated recording of information. **Business English** is not just a book, it is a concept where the physical object is intended to underline for the user the purpose for which (s)he is using it.

It is for this reason that the book is produced on nice quality paper, with sophisticated printing and the possibility of using a loose leaf format. All of these are not gimmicks but are intended to encourage the language learner to see the **organising** of the new material as an **important part** of the learning process, and the arranging of it in such a way that it can be re-accessed as an essential part of the process of recording.

The basic idea of **Business English** is that the student provides the content, and the teacher provides the language. The book itself provides the sophisticated formats which make possible this change of emphasis.

2. THE ROLE OF THE TEACHER

Business English is not a conventional business coursebook. The aim is not directly to **teach** but to provide material that invites the student to think about **what** he or she needs to learn, and to begin working on it. It is an individualised learning programme designed to provide learner training in the form of a language study project (see page 17 below). In a group context this means that the book does not provide structured tasks in the form of group activities, but instead challenges the students to find **their own** ways of helping each other to work through it and embark on individual learning programmes. Rather than being full of exercises with answers, and activities with a pre-designed outcome, the book represents an **open-ended** task, pre-determining neither the manner nor the anticipated outcome with which it is approached.

The role of the teacher is **not** to provide a rigidly sequenced orchestration of the book through a sense of structured activities, nor just to use the book piecemeal as a source of teaching material, but to:

– Clearly devolve the task of working through the book to the student(s).

– Explain that only this ground rule can enable the students to treat classroom work as if it were a real business task with real business communication.

– Ensure that, as far as possible, discussion of the task and the project is conducted along the lines, and using the language, of business and professional meetings.

– Act as **consultant** for the students by providing guidelines, proposals, and tools for the students to use in working together.

– Act as language **auditor**. This means listening for mis- and missing collocational lexis in the language they use to approach the task; training the students to identify and record language both from the material of the book and from the teacher.

– Directing group activities when necessary to stimulate and motivate the energy of the group, provide variety of pace, or model certain activities.

In one-to-one work this is not a difficult role to fulfil, and the book itself provides a framework, together with the approaches suggested in *One-to-One: A Teacher's Handbook, Peter Wilberg, LTP 1987*. But just as no two individuals are the same, so also will no two groups be the same. For the one-to-one teacher it is easier to maintain an open-ended approach. In a class the teacher must pay more attention to role, both acting as participant/consultant in businesslike group planning, and like any other participant, exercising leadership when necessary.

As consultant and auditor to the group the teacher will be required to provide expertise in the following areas:

1. Suggesting structures (eg pair work, feedback sessions etc). Suggesting but not imposing ... remember that the classes are best conducted as business meetings.

2. Suggesting different arrangements for the physical layout of the room for drills, group discussion, presentations, pair- or small group work.

3. Organising and auditing student presentations.

4. Ensuring the availability of a wide variety of supplementary authentic material for use by the students: company brochures, colour magazines, video recordings, dictionaries etc.

5. Suggesting and organising the use of cassette recordings.

6. Suggesting homework: pre-reading units and making notes for discussions or presentations, doing self-study drills, writing activities etc.

CLASSROOM ENGLISH

Teachers are strongly urged to read and think about Page 7. We believe that in many small group courses, it will be appropriate for one or two days 'lessons', to be conducted as 'meetings'. Either the teacher or a student may take the chair, but the purpose of this meeting – not to be confused with a simulation which may also form part of the course – is twofold:

– to break down the teacher-student relationship, and help build up a more professional relationship between teacher and student.

– to provide an ideal opportunity to practise language which is essential for the student after the course, rather than the relatively useless language which typifies most student-teacher exchanges.

Approaching some of the lessons in the style of meetings, as suggested on Page 7, can give the student an impression of a well-prepared and well-thought-out course, suited to his or her needs. We emphasise that we strongly believe that professional courses should meet the professional on his or her home territory, rather than reducing this competent professional to the level of a dependent pupil simply because the client has a less than adequate grasp of English.

3. WHAT LEVEL IS BUSINESS ENGLISH?

All traditional language teaching books state their level reasonably clearly. This is not possible with **Business English**. However strange it may appear, we believe that **Business English** can be used with students from post-beginners to advanced. There are three reasons for this:

1. Social Language

Experience shows that almost all business students require a much greater range of social English than they have from any form of school English teaching. It is simple to say that a business person needs a repertoire of expressions to communicate the simple message 'No'. It is quite a different thing for the student to build up such a repertoire. Elementary students need such a repertoire, and need to start from not knowing the expressions. However, many quite advanced students, while able to generate expressions, do not generate **natural** expressions and may not have a true feel for the force of what they say. In short, their requirements in this area are very similar to students at a much lower level of general English. As a result, the open format pages of the Social Language Organiser section of **Business English** can be used by students at widely different levels, though the information they record will differ from student to student.

2. Formula phrases

In many cases large quantities of business language is very stylised – the language of the telephone, welcome speeches, formal meetings, presentations, etc. Low level students do not have this language, and experience has shown us that even quite advanced students, able to generate the **content** of what they say in a meeting or presentation, are frequently at a serious disadvantage because they do not have the **formula phrases needed to provide the framework** of such business activities. This is reflected by a number of pages in **Business English** which simply present this language for study and, if desired by the student, learned by heart. However unexciting this may be, it represents a real need for a very wide range of levels for the business English student.

3. Word partnerships

Finally, working with large numbers of students of this type has shown that even those whose general English is upper intermediate, have a serious language defect. The term 'upper intermediate' usually implies that they have a good vocabulary, and can generate a wide range of sentences with a high degree of grammatical accuracy. Unfortunately, they frequently do not have the ability to bring vocabulary and grammar together effectively in the language used in business. A simple example will suffice to illustrate this. We asked a large number of such students to identify the verbs which they thought they could use with the noun *'meeting'*. Even students whose general level of English was quite high, produced only the following: *go to, attend, assist at/to(!), make(!),* and, for the better students, *have.* They simply did not see the possibility of combinations such as; *cancel a meeting, set up a meeting, wind up a meeting, chair a meeting,* etc.

The result is that a large part of the content of **Business English** is designed to help students improve their power to make these collocations (which are called **word**

partnerships in the book itself). Two sections of the book are specifically designed to help students identify and record partnerships helpful to them in their own business area. This material, too, will be useful to students at a very wide range of levels.

SYLLABUS IMPLICATIONS

The implications for difference of level are that students whose general level of English is low will acquire substantial power to communicate, through the ability to produce useful and effective word partnerships, but they will frequently make grammatical mistakes when using these partnerships. In other words, their English may be **defective**, but it will almost certainly be **effective.** This is one of the compromises needed in in-service business English courses – perhaps the most important one – which we discussed earlier.

For higher level students, the ability to make natural word partnerships will increase their communicative power, and, as a result of the level of their general English, they will make many fewer mistakes.

In short, **Business English** represents a real attempt to bring a lexical syllabus (see below) into business and ESP teaching. The basis of this syllabus is not improving the student's vocabulary, nor indeed improving grammar as in a traditional course. It is improving the ability to **combine** grammar and vocabulary – increased **collocational power** – which will make these students' English more effective, even if it remains grammatically defective.

This combination of factors means that **Business English** can be used with students whose general English covers a very wide range of levels. The book is constructed so that student(s) and teacher(s) can **negotiate** together about those pages which are of most use for the individual student or class. On a principle similar to the kind of personal organiser which many of these students may have, students are invited to use particular sections which are more closely associated with their own needs, and to give less emphasis, or even to ignore, pages which lie outside the scope of their needs, bearing in mind such factors as their level of English, linguistic needs, and practical considerations such as the length and intensity of the course they are following.

Unlike traditional business English course books, **Business English** has designed into it the solution to the compromises which are a necessary part of this kind of course.

4. THE LEXICAL APPROACH TO BUSINESS ENGLISH

Business English represents a radically new approach to language analysis, syllabus design and materials writing for both general and business English teaching. We call this approach 'lexical' not because it excludes grammar and functions, but because it grounds both of these in the **words** the student needs to learn. To describe a language is to describe the way words go together in that language. The common co-occurrence of certain words with one another has up till now been referred to as "collocation". However, the term "collocation" has been mainly used to describe a marginal set of idiomatic word combinations such as *deeply moved* or *execute a will* in which one or both partners in the combination tend regularly to co-occur with one another, imposing an almost automatic association of words in the native speaker's mind.

A quick review of this very text you are reading, however, will demonstrate the point that co-occurrence is by no means a marginal idiomatic phenomenon but one determined by the specific language field or sub-language in question; *language analysis, syllabus design* and, *business English* are not "common" collocations but nevertheless occur with great frequency when talking about EFL. *Election forecast/results/victory* are part of the topical language of politics. In a sense there is no such thing as "general English" at all, but instead a set of topical, situational, professional and technical sub-languages, each of which relies heavily on a finite set of collocations.

MIS-COLLOCATIONS AND MISSING COLLOCATIONS

Our interest in collocational analysis was aroused by many years of one-to-one teaching of foreign business executives, which clearly demonstrated the importance of the distiction between so-called "overt" and "covert" error. Overt errors are mistakes made by the student in the English that (s)he uses. These mistakes can generally be identified as **mis-collocations** of one or more words. Covert error is language that the student fails to use or does not have at his or her disposal to use. Experience of this type of error suggests it almost always consists of **missing collocations** in the student's language.

To give an example: "We discussed about the possibility to sell our product in the United States." Most teachers can readily recognize the principal mistakes here: the wrong use of the preposition; and the wrong use of the infinitive "to sell". The prepositional error is a classic miscollocation of the word *discuss*. The error . . . any error . . . involves at least two words which are combined wrongly. The word *discuss* collocates with *something;* it collocates not with a specific word like *about* but with specific **word types** (a noun, or noun phrase).

No amount of "general English" lessons on prepositions can substitute for learning to use this specific verb in correct collocation with other words. Instead of categorizing student mistakes in abstract linguistic terms (like 'prepositions', or 'present perfect') we need to listen very carefully to what they are trying to say and how this would normally be said, in the situations for which they are preparing.

In this case we would then realise that replacing the wrongly used infinitive with a gerund ("discuss the possibilities of selling . .") though providing a grammatically well-formed result, could by no means be reckoned to be teaching the student the English they need. *"Ways of selling* would be a better expression; *US sales prospects,* an expression made entirely of nouns, would be the **professional** substitute for the verb phrase employed by the student. (see **Business English,** page 59).

Let us consider the language needed to talk about football as an example. The lexis of this sub-language cannot be defined by any list of single words; instead it consists of a well-defined set of verb-noun collocations such as *score a goal, kick/pass/head the ball,* etc. The most important collocation type is the **verb-noun** partnership, for this **completes** the other types; *final score* is a useful adjective-noun collocation for talking about football, but its use is limited without an appropriate verb such as *give, see, hear.*

The problem with the structural approach was that it started with verb structures, and made vocabulary something additional. We propose **starting with important individualised** lexical collocations, particularly verb-noun pairs, around which more complex language is then built.

A core collocation such as *adjust a valve* is formed from the overlap of two lexical fields: the fields of possible partners to each of *adjust* and *valve,* for example *adjust the fitting* or *close the valve.* Each partner in the core collocation is itself a "keyword" with its own set of possible collocational partners, determined by usage and terminology within the sub-language of which it forms a part.

Students need to know these fields and the **word partnerships** (the term we use in **Business English** in place of the jargon word *collocation*) they contain, to provide the basis for working with more complex sentence structures.

5. GENERATING A WORD PARTNERSHIP LIST

A list of word partnerships needed by an individual student can be generated in different ways: it can be generated by reformulation: listening and noting the missing collocations in the students output; or it can be generated from a text by several means:

a. Asking students to underline or highlight the word partnerships they find (prompting them with some that are already underlined).

b. Preparing a gapped list of collocations, so that the students must find the partner word for each item either from a written text or as a listening exercise.

c. By co-dictation, in which two texts and/or two lists are used. In one text or list one half of each partnership is gapped, and in the other text or list the other half is gapped. By jointly reading the text/list without seeing each other's version, they must fill the gaps in either text or list.

It is essential for teachers (and useful for students) to be able to identify different collocational types. This can be done as follows:

i. By highlighting sample word partnerships in a text in different colours according to collocational types and getting the students to use coloured pens and find more examples of each.

ii. By using highlighter pens or ballpens to mark or underline the word partnerships on a two-column list according to collocational type.

iii. By having specially prepared pages for recording the three major types of collocation (**verb-noun, adjective-noun,** and **noun-noun, Business English** pp 50/52).

6. A PRODUCT-ORIENTATED COURSE

As far as possible, we believe that language courses for professionals should be constructed on project lines – early in the course the student, teacher and institution should negotiate objectives, set deadlines etc. Throughout the course, objectives should be reviewed and new deadlines set in a process of constant negotiation between student and teacher. We believe this is most likely to be effective, and appeal to the business person if, whenever possible, a definite **product** is proposed which will be **produced to a deadline.**

In a few cases, where students come from a similar background, for example the same company, it may be possible to have as an objective to produce a short, well-produced 4-page leaflet or brochure describing that company, a particular product etc. All of the work should, directly or less directly, contribute towards this concrete course product.

In the case of most students, however, we believe that it will be more satisfactory for the product to be an oral presentation. This is particularly the case for one-to-one students. Most business people, at some stage of their career, do require to present parts of their organisation, products, a report, figures etc. The presentation involves many different aspects, among which we may mention:

1. The language of presentation – stereotyped phrases for structuring any presentation (see BE Pages 130/131).

2. The content of the presentation will largely be represented by important word partnerships, and probably the grammar of change (BE appropriate Pages 58 to 76, and 84 to 95).

3. Presentation skills – in particular the ability to speak to a fairly large room, projecting to the back of the room. We believe this could replace conventional 'pronunciation practice' on professional courses.

4. Appropriate visuals – most presentations are supported by material on the overhead projector. The students could, during their course, prepare appropriate visuals either by photocopying helpful pages from **Business English** onto transparency, or by typing and photocopying material of their own.

We hope it is clear from the above suggestions, that we see the production of a written report, or a preparation and performance of a full oral presentation, as a way of focussing students' attention, and providing a focus and orientation **during** a course which can otherwise seem as if they are learning professional language only because it might be useful to them **later**.

It is worth commenting that some students on professional language courses in fact do not have heavily business-orientated language needs. This does not mean that they cannot do a presentation. Students can choose a presentation from a very wide range of topics – from the most business orientated, to very relaxed and more personal topics. To assist teachers, we reproduce on pages 52 and 53 of this manual lists of potential presentation topics as proposed in Peter Wilberg's book *One to One, Language Teaching Publications 1987*.

7. STARTING A COURSE – DAY ONE

We assume most students using **Business English** will be on relatively short, intensive in-service courses. For convenience we describe the possible content of a first day programme – assuming, perhaps, that contact hours are from 9–12 and from 2–5.

In most cases, the course has probably been preceded by some form of needs analysis sent to the student, or possibly the student's employer, prior to the course. This, together with the student's application form, and any information received from student or employer, should have been studied by the teacher in advance to provide the basis for a first-day interview. As suggested elsewhere in this Manual (see Page 21) we suggest that an integral part of the course should be identifying the student's language needs, the setting and revising of objectives etc. This clearly has an important role to play on the morning of Day 1, and we suggest teachers may want to begin by using **Needs 1 – Topics** and **Needs 2 – Functions**, Pages 10 and 11.

After doing this, it may be appropriate to ask the student to read through Pages 5 and 6, and to check that the student has available all the language needed on Pages 7 (for lower level students pronunciation of some of the important expressions is essential).

Depending on the length and intensity of the course, and personality factors for the student and teacher, it may be appropriate to do a little more work on the Needs – perhaps Page 13 **Daily Routine.**

As discussed elsewhere (in discussing Section 4 and 5) we suggest that Day 1 should also introduce the important idea of Word Partnerships – either before or after looking at appropriate resource texts. As a basic plan, we propose using Pages 57/59, and perhaps one additional Key word page, possibly in conjunction with Pages 138/139, then, if time permits, apply this to an appropriate professional text, by first asking the student to read Page 45 (or in the case of very low level students, discussing and explaining the content of Page 45 for the student), and then using the headlines from such texts as the day's issue of the Financial Times, or an appropriate professional journal or company brochure.

The other point which we believe it is important to introduce at the early stage of the course is to discuss the students' and teacher's attitude to mistakes. This can be done by referring to the note at the top of Page 120.

We stress that it is important to remember that all students arrive with fairly strong expectations of what their course will be like. Any course which simply runs counter to their expectations is likely to be unhelpful. It is important, therefore, that the teacher approaches the first morning with a view to **negotiating** the course content, and style and emphases of the work, **with the student(s).** We believe the pages suggested here will provide a sound basis for covering the key issues on Day 1.

8. BUILDING A COURSE WITH BUSINESS ENGLISH

We assume that most courses using **Business English** will be relatively short, relatively intensive in-service professional courses. Naturally, as with all other courses, the objective must be to provide a variety of activities which will result in a balanced course. Many less experienced teachers are used, on teacher training courses, to the idea of a balanced **lesson** – we would suggest that for these courses the unit of the course which needs to be balanced is probably the work done on a particular **day**. In most cases this will either be a full day – perhaps up to 6 or 8 contact hours, or a half-day. In either case, we believe you will find it easiest to plan an effective course if you try to maintain some balance in the work done on each day. Three points need to be made:

1. In addition to any daily structure there is also an overall structure. We suggest elsewhere that it is a good idea for such courses to adopt a project approach, producing either written material or an oral presentation at the end of a week or at the end of the course. Clearly any daily structure needs to take account of this longer-term course structure.

2. In general, there should be a movement throughout the course from the relatively early days, which will be much more heavily teacher directed, to the later days where the programme, order of material, speed etc. should be much more dictated by the autonomous student(s). One of the main purposes of the material in **Business English** is to provide a 'course plan' to undermine the idea of the teacher as directing activities which have correct answers. The material is deliberately designed to encourage and support student autonomy. This should be reflected in the day-to-day course planning.

3. Teachers who are familiar with traditional course books must recognise that **Business English** is very different. Most course books, and indeed many supplementary materials, are designed so that one unit, or one page, may be taught in one lesson. This is absolutely not the case with **Business English**. Indeed, nothing could be further from the truth. **Business English** is a combination of course book, course plan, work book and course record. All of the following types of work should be seen as quite normal with this radically different material:

a. The student referring to several pages, in different sections, in a single lesson (for example, Pages 20, 94, 130/131).

b. Students using the same page several times during the course (for example, Pages 11, 40, 67, 136/137).

c. Students using a particular page regularly, to record similar information for convenience of recall (many pages, including, for example, Pages 50/56, 81/83, 108/126).

d. Students using the same page twice for different reasons (for example the Word Partnership pages).

e. Recording the same information on two different pages (Pages 88/89, and 116/117).

f. Students reading an introductory page before working on material of that kind with the teacher (for example Pages 16, 138/139, 147).

g. Students preparing or revising a page without teacher supervision – 'homework'.

h. Students using a small group of pages in a way similar to a conventional course book unit (for example the Needs pages to revise objectives, or Pages 84/93 to prepare Pages 94/95 for later oral presentation).

Elsewhere in this Teachers' Manual you will find many suggestions for activities which are preparatory to, or follow up to actual use of the book (see pages 42 to 50). We must emphasise that we believe that a lot of teacher-contact-time will not involve direct use of the book. Students will, in addition, use resource texts, do oral practices suggested by the material, but perhaps based on a reference grammar, discuss freely with the teacher (though this may result in material subsequently being recorded in **Business English**), etc.

There is a general principle of good teaching – Teach the Student, not the Material. All teachers familiar with general English will remember 'trying to finish the exercise before the end of the lesson', or even trying to finish a book before the end of the course. When this happens, it usually means the material is completed unsatisfactorily, and the interests of the material are put above those of the student! **Business English** is conceptualised to put students' needs and student autonomy at the centre of the course. A natural consequence of this is that the printed materials are intended to **support** student and teacher, and should at no time dominate. There is no need to 'finish' anything; the primary objective should always be to satisfy the students' linguistic and personal needs so that the course will be of use long after it is over.

9. THE SECTIONS IN BUSINESS ENGLISH

Business English is not divided into units, but into sections. The sections may be approached in any order, although most courses will probably want to use the first section, **Needs**, early in the course. It is also possible to omit sections completely, do them partially, and, within a section, to take the material in the order best suited to the individual student.

1. LANGUAGE LEARNING ORGANISER

Most business English courses involve a pre-course needs analysis, sent to the student or client before the course. Experience shows that, however necessary these may be from a PR point of view, they are often of little help in deciding course content. Not infrequently the first morning or day on an intensive business course involves further needs analysis, with the teacher working with the individual students. There is a temptation to rush this activity so that "the real teaching" can begin. We suggest that this is a mistake. Indeed, we suggest needs analysis should not **precede** the course, but be a **fully integrated** part of the course. Clearly, it will be given more emphasis at the beginning of the course, where teacher and students negotiate and set course objectives, but it should be natural to return to the needs analysis pages to review progress, and revise objectives throughout the course.

Note that the pages have been carefully designed so that much of the language the student needs to state his or her needs is provided on the page. It is the student's task to **recycle** that language to the appropriate parts of the page, adding, if necessary, personal details.

For low level students, it is important to make clear to them that they can complete the needs analysis pages either in English, using the language provided, or, if necessary, in their own language. It is essential that students realise that **these pages are in no sense a test,** but are to help them and the teacher to **identify as clearly as possible the language most likely to be helpful.**

The pages are intended to produce a cost effective course, and teachers may like to point this feature out to students. When using **Business English**, teachers are constantly encouraged to use the kind of language familiar to the business person (*cost effective*) rather than sticking to the language common to language teachers (*needs analysis*).

Notice that this section contains a great deal of language which will be of immediate use to the student, and, as such, is a fully integrated part of the course. The student who liaises with the Japanese subsidiary of his firm will, almost inevitably, require the word *liaise* (see Page 13).

There is an important point to be made – in doing the needs analysis pages there are two possibilities – the students **know** the English provided (words such as *liaise*), in which case they can recycle them into the appropriate sections on these pages. Alternatively, students do **not** know the language on these pages – in this case a real and immediate language need has been determined – the language which will allow the student to express his or her language needs!

In common with other sections throughout **Business English** this section has brief notes which provide 'expert help' (see BE Page 8). It is important that teachers are familiar with these notes in advance, as the notes are intended to **endorse what the teacher says to the students**, and to ensure that all concerned – student, teacher and material are "pulling in the same direction" to ensure a course which is both relaxed and efficient.

2.   PERSONAL LANGUAGE ORGANISER

This short section is particularly intended for students whose English is of a relatively low level. However much students think they are going to use "business English", it is important for them to realise that they also need to be able to talk about themselves, colleagues, and interests. This section is also intended to provide some variety, particularly for one-to-one classes. It is not possible to spend all day on such courses doing "heavy" professional language; this section provides an opportunity for something more personal.

The section has three main uses:

a.   To provide a certain face validity for the student. As previously mentioned one of the purposes of the book is to support the teacher and school's choice of course programme. However serious or intensive the course is supposed to be, **Business English** suggests that more personal language should be a natural and integrated part of any business course.

b.   It provides material to facilitate the personal relationship between teacher and student, particularly on one-to-one and small group courses. Some of the material (see particularly Pages 24, 25, 26) is deliberately more light-hearted and, as such, suitable as a counterbalance for some of the more serious language work.

c.   Closer to the more strictly ESP element of **Business English**, Pages 20 to 23 ensure that students think about their company and colleagues, and can describe them clearly and acceptably in English.

Two column format

In common with many pages of **Business English**, a number of pages in this section are divided into a notional two column format (see Pages 18, 21, 24). On the whole, students are invited to complete material which is in a column to the left, with their own writing to the right. This formatting allows students to revise by masking the right-hand column, and checking that they can recall the material they recorded earlier.

We suggest that different pages of this section are used from time to time throughout any course. In general we think that it is unlikely that any teacher or student would want to work through this section page-by-page.

A number of more advanced students may not want to do some of the pages of this section, but we would strongly recommend that all students use Pages 20/23.

3. SOCIAL LANGUAGE ORGANISER

This section is one of the most important in **Business English**. Every student, at all levels, requires a comprehensive repertoire of language for dealing with a wide range of social situations. A great deal of business depends not on negotiating skills, or complex deals, but on efficient social communication. Do you trust the other person? Do you have a positive impression of the other person? Can you make a visitor feel comfortable? These are some of the central questions for any business person. Accordingly, this section will probably play a major part in most business English courses, though the emphasis would differ according to the level, interests and objectives of individual students.

Most of this section suggests that students should build up a **repertoire of expressions with which they feel comfortable**. It may be necessary for some students to demonstrate for them that simply "saying what you mean" is not sufficient. Teachers may find the following example useful:

Could I speak to Mr. Richards please?
No.
Have you despatched my order yet?
No.
Are you happy with the 30% discount?
No.

In these examples, even if the answer is *"Yes"*, the effect of a one-word answer is to convey abruptness, unhappiness, and possibly even the exact opposite of the overt message. All European students will readily recognise this, and students from further afield (for example Japan) are well aware that "saying what you mean" is only the beginning of communication skills in business English.

For low level students, there is an obvious danger of overload. How many ways of saying 'No' do they need? Will they be using English predominantly with native speakers (British or American) or predominantly with other non-natives? In the latter case, a smaller repertoire of such expressions may be quite adequate.

It is also important that students feel comfortable saying the individual expressions they record. Although the expression *"I am sorry, I am afraid that's not very convenient"* is totally natural (British) English, no student will use it unless he or she "feels right" when saying it. This is partly a matter of having heard this or similar expressions, and partly a matter of having **heard yourself** saying it a number of times. This is why repetition, and ultimately audio-recording of the language students record in their books, is suggested.

However, it is not the teacher's task to tell the students how to behave; the teacher's role is to try, clearly and as explicitly as possible, to explain to the student the **effect** he or she creates by using particular language. The teacher is, in effect, **a monitor of the student's language**, who can provide instant feedback. Again it may be helpful to remind teachers that many students attempt high levels of accuracy on courses which are much too short. In these circumstances, it is helpful to bear in mind the difference between **effective** and **defective** communication.

Many of the pages in this section have the **two-column format** discussed above (see Pages 30, 37, 39, 41). In general, the idea is that students should record in such a way that, after an appropriate time gap (days during a course, or after returning home) they can mask the right-hand column and check that they can recall the language that they have recorded.

In some cases they are asked to record **equivalents** in their own language (Your Language – English pages 30–33). In these cases, the normal procedure will be that they **observe** a natural English expression – this may be used by the teacher, or be noted in some input materials – text book, video, TV etc. After recording the English, students should search for an expression in their own language which "feels the same" (has the same illocutionary force); it is important that students are not looking for a quick "translation". Think, for example, of the difference between a lightly and quickly said '*No, no, no, no, that's quite all right*' and '*No. That's all right*', said rather more slowly, with a pause after the '*No*'.

On some occasions it may be appropriate that the student wants to express an idea in his or her own language and the teacher needs to try several English expressions before finding something which student and teacher can agree is an equivalent with which the student feels comfortable. It is important here to accept that negotiating with the student – **searching together** for language which the student agrees is, and will be useful, is more important that simply filling up the book indiscriminately.

A number of the pages in this section cross-refer to material elsewhere in the book, in particular:

Pages 28–37 refer to Being Diplomatic, pages 81–83
Saying '*Yes*' and Saying '*No*' relate to Section 8, particularly pages 151, 159
'Would' is taken up again under business grammar, see pages 78/9
Several Word Lobsters could relate to Presentations (pages 130/131).

Some additional points about this section need to be made:

a. Teachers must not underestimate the importance of sheer repetition for the student. With new language which feels uncomfortable, students should be encouraged to repeat the same expression aloud several times. Hearing yourself say something can persuade that it sounds and feels natural. Rather than making this pure repetition, teachers are encouraged to help students see it as a preparation ('pronunciation practice') prior to recording the language for subsequent revision work.

b. Much of this section should be very much in the teacher's mind during the course, particularly in one-to-one or small group teaching. That teaching situation – two people talking together, or one person talking to a very small group – closely resembles situations in which many students will wish to use English in business. The teacher should attempt to capitalise on this by **consciously incorporating** a lot of language useful to the student in his or her (the teacher's) own language use. This means the teacher should consciously look to say '*Yes*' or '*No*' or to make appropriate 'noises' while the student is speaking and then, draw the student's attention explicitly to the language that has been used.

It will easily be seen that this means the teacher should, as far as possible, try to break down the teacher/student relationship, and aim more for a business person/consultant relationship. If this latter relationship is successfully established, much of the language required for this section will occur naturally without the teacher having to contrive its introduction.

c.   The language needed to fill in the 'heads' of the Word Lobsters (Pages 41/44) should be language which the student and teacher agree would be useful as a result of work done in class. It could easily tie in with preparing a presentation (see also Page 130).

d.   The Restaurant pages (Pages 38/39) could be used as the basis of a more relaxed conversation lesson. A conversation about food, followed by attempts to describe some local specialities, could result in the student recording brief descriptions after unsuccessful attempts, consultation with the teacher, dictionary work etc.

In some cases it may be appropriate for students actually to practise hosting a visit to a restaurant. If this is possible and practical it should be done in a proper, business-like way with, for example, the teacher role-playing the part of a visiting business partner. It may provide some variety in the diet of the average EFL teacher if (s)he is entertained for a business lunch by a visiting German or Scandinavian executive!

e.   The three speeches (Page 40) are intended to give students the confidence of knowing that, if they use the language **exactly** as given here, they will sound right, natural and effective. In our experience very few students feel comfortable in the situations suggested by these three speeches. The language may, therefore, need to be practised regularly. We are prepared to suggest that students who feel it would be useful to them might like to deliver one of the speeches **each day** during an intensive course, or one each week on a course lasting for a longer period. The fact that each one needs to be done several times is not boring repetition – native speakers of English only feel comfortable with these situations when they have done them again and again.

It is also important to realise that these speeches are useless if they are mumbled. Teachers may think it is more appropriate for many of their business students to ask students to 'deliver' one of these speeches on a regular basis – in a fairly large room, and at a comfortable volume, rather than doing conventional 'pronunciation practice'.

Linguists now tell us that native speakers have a very large repertoire of learned sentences – things which require no mental activity to produce, but are simply recalled, whole, from the memory. While this does not make for exciting teaching, it does suggest that we may need to encourage students to learn this kind of language in a more parrot-fashion way than we would perhaps hope. It is worth remembering that in these situations, which are often socially sensitive, a key factor to feeling comfortable is confidence. If the person delivering the speech is sure that the language they are using is correct and appropriate, they will feel comfortable, project well, and create the positive atmosphere and impression which they intend. We urge teachers not to underestimate the value of encouraging students to practise these speeches again and again.

4. RESOURCE TEXT ORGANISER

Many teachers working in the field of business English and ESP are worried that however confident they are as teachers, they do not have the necessary background knowledge to teach bankers, insurance brokers etc. This section is carefully designed to ensure that the teacher's professional language skills can be used to help the student extract language useful to the individual student from appropriate professional texts (usually printed, but also audio or video, if available).

Too often language teaching has resorted to using the same methodology with professional texts as it has employed with the general interest text found in conventional course books. This has usually meant focusing on a particular grammar point exemplified in the text and extracting useful vocabulary ('Are there any words you don't understand?). We have found this grammar/vocabulary distinction frequently does not help students and is, at best, a very inefficient way of helping students on in-service ESP courses.

Collocation

One of the most important theoretical insights which underlies the radically new approach in **Business English** is the importance, particularly in professional English, of **collocations**, words which regularly occur together. In **Business English** we have called these 'Word Partnerships' as part of our general strategy of using terminology likely to be accessible and usable by the student rather than requiring students to learn jargon from language teachers' terminology.

A great deal of thought, observation, and experimentation has gone into this key element of **Business English**. The most important pages to provide an introduction to the idea are pages 57/59 and 138/139 We have found, quite simply, that students frequently have a large repertoire of nouns at their disposal but do not know the words which collocate and, most particularly, they do not have the collocating verbs.

Not 'word lists'

Every teacher is familiar with the students' urge, or perhaps even need, to write word lists in which one word in the student's own language corresponds to one word in English. Part of the purpose of **Business English** is to undermine this assumption. Many pages of the book encourage students to record **whole phrases, complete sentences** or **word partnerships**. A fundamental problem arises if they are to do this—where are they to get the language from? The basic answer is by observation. We suggest students should be searching through, or '**auditing**' professional texts, both recorded and printed, for language which students and teacher think would be useful. Section 4 directs students to different kinds of language which can be found in resource texts, and provides carefully formatted pages for the language to be recorded in the most useful way. As usual, there is a notional two column format through most of the pages to ensure that students can check recall at a later stage by masking the second column.

Word Partnerships

It is important to notice that many of the word partnerships students may wish to find are 'obvious' to a native speaker – they may be simple noun-noun pairs such as *market confidence* or multi-word time expressions such as *during the last quarter of the fiscal year*. Such combinations are much less obvious to the non-native speaker and therefore to the learner. **Training students to audit texts for useful language by underlining appropriate and useful word partnerships is an important element of the course plan we propose.**

It is important to note that some important verb-noun partnerships may not occur as consecutive words in the resource text, for example, *the meeting had been set up by the Germans, but the French pulled out at the last minute*. Here, the relevant word partnerships are *to set up a meeting, to pull out of a meeting*. Once again the teacher's knowledge of English will allow them to audit text relatively easily. One of the main objectives of in-service ESP courses should be to pass that skill on to the students, so that both during, and perhaps most importantly, after the course, students can acquire language efficiently from the kind of professional texts that they come into contact with in their daily work.

Although we have included the Resource Text Organiser as Section 4 in the book, in other words before the Word Partnership Organiser, teachers may prefer to introduce the idea of word partnerships before approaching the idea of particular texts as resource materials. On a one or two week intensive course we would suggest that the first morning might well be given to using Section 1, and the afternoon to doing pages 57/9 and perhaps one other page of Section 6, plus perhaps pages 138/139. The ordering of the materials is more a psychological than a pedagogical question. For students who are relaxed and co-operative, the above plan may be best. If the student's whole attitude is workaholic, it may be better to push through the needs section a little more quickly and then introduce one or two authentic professional texts ('Now we can get down to some real work'), and then take a little longer to introduce the idea of word partnerships as being a more useful and efficient way of tackling the texts than simply rushing in to check understanding, and mine the text for grammar and vocabulary. It must be remembered, however, that many students will arrive on such courses with strong expectations of what they **think** will be useful to them. It would be unwise to ignore their expectations and simply plunge into a new approach, however successful that approach might be.

In small group teaching, and particularly in one-to-one, the establishing of confidence and rapport is a very important part of the first day's work. We suggest that working with the student on one or two pages from Section 1 during the first couple of hours should give a fairly clear indication of whether it is best to move on to introducing the idea of word partnerships or whether it is better to introduce some formal text work until the student unwinds, and teacher and student have reached an understanding of the best way to develop an efficient and enjoyable course.

An important part of the formatting of the pages of **Business English** is to help students to record information for convenience of checking and recall later. We are here suggesting that resource texts should be used as a **source of collocations**, rather than grammar or vocabulary separately. It is, therefore, natural to record the collocations in a two column format so that, as elsewhere in the book, the students can later check their recall by masking the one column.

It is also worth noting that asking students to record different kinds of collocation on different pages (verb-noun, or noun-noun combinations) is a disguised grammar exercise. When the material was being tested, we found that students frequently knew one use of the word – *wholesale* or *initial* as adjectives but not verbs, etc. One of the ways to producing greater levels of fluency and more effective language use is to encourage students to know the different grammatical roles particular words may play. It is for this reason that the **grammar of the word**, rather than the grammar of the sentence, is such a strong feature of the design behind **Business English**.

THINGS YOU CAN DO WITH WORD PARTNERSHIP LISTS

a. Ranking or sequencing.

This can be done on the basis of word-partnership lists which describe stages in a process, elements in a plan or timetable, the description of a daily routine, points on an agenda etc. Having presented or generated the list, the students then rank the items in order or priority or importance, or sequence them in time.

b. Expanding.

Word-partnerships can be expanded linguistically by brainstorming more partners for either word within each collocation. They can also be expanded **thematically**. A job description or technical process for example, contains major elements or stages which can be broken down into a set of subsidiary elements or stages.

c. Adding sentence heads.

Job and process descriptions, daily routines, timetables, plans and flow charts etc, are all **action sequences** which have at their heart a set of verb-noun partnerships. The same applies to story lines and events, memos and reports. After listing these, sentence heads can be added; These can be either question heads *(Do you, How often do you)* or function heads *(I must, We need to)*.

d. Sorting

Word-partnerships may be sorted any number of ways; not only by collocational type but also topically, by synonymy of meaning, by pronounciation, or by grammatical similarity, eg those followed by the . . .*ing* form of the verb.

e. Binary transcription

This means breaking down a sentence into a set of collocated word partnerships and transcribing the sentence **vertically** in two columns. To begin with, the word partnerships may be extracted or dictated out-of-sequence in the left-hand column for the student(s) to re-order; besides its value as a "jigsaw" exercise, binary transcription is a powerful tool for training students in identifying and chaining both lexical and syntactic collocations.

f. Gapped transcription

A gapped transcription can be used as the basis of a listening task: "collocational cloze".

> The easily– .... multi– .... combining pipe-plug and ball– .... in one .... is immediately .... from our regular ....

Here are some further suggestions

– Sort them into groups (verb-noun, adjective-noun, noun-noun)

– Define a collocation with further collocations (**apply for a job:** fill in a form, write a letter, wait for a reply, go for an interview etc).

– Identify Keywords (prepositions or nouns which go with more than one verb, or verbs that go with more than one noun, or preposition).

– Ask students to **change** one word in each pair (arrange a meeting ➤ arrange an appointment).

– Make three-word partnerships from two-word collocations by adding a third word either before, after, or between the partner-words. (Most typically, inserting an adjective in verb-noun combinations).

– Invent communicative drills for pairwork, for example one student calling out a collocation so that another can respond with an echo question:

S1: Do the shopping.
S2: Do **what?**
S1: The **shopping**.
S2: Oh I see. Do the shopping.

5. WORD PARTNERSHIP ORGANISER

This section represents the most innovative material in **Business English**, and the greatest theoretical step forward. As we have already mentioned, many business students have a large vocabulary, particularly of nouns, but are unable to make sentences around the nouns. In itself, this is something of a theoretical surprise. Traditionally the 'most important word' in a sentence is thought to be either the subject or the verb. We are suggesting that, for many business sentences, the most important word for determining the content of the sentence, and therefore the content of a business English course, is the **object**. A moment's thought reveals why this is so – the most usual subjects in spoken business English in its narrower sense are probably *I, We, The Company*. Not suprisingly, these are not particularly helpful in allowing us to identify the sort of language students need. However, in sentences like *We have just received a wholesale order from Germany,* the key word is clearly *order*. If a student wants to talk about orders, the essential language needed is the collocating verbs and adjectives. Learning the words which do (and do **not**) go together, and how they go together, is easier, more useful, and more effective for in-service business students than further studies of traditional grammar (but see also particularly pp 78/95). We strongly suggest that the idea of word partnerships is introduced to students as early as possible in their course (but see comment in Section 4 above). The idea is probably best introduced using Pages 57/9, combined with pages 138/139.

Although the section is innovative and extensive, each page follows a similar format. The teacher should, however, note the following points:

a.   Many of the background words belong to **two** grammatical groups (an **initial** order, to **initial** an order; a sales **increase**, to **increase** sales). In the first part of each activity where students are asked to underline the words dividing them into two groups, **it is important to check that students have underlined some of the words twice, in different colours**. Part of the process of making students' English more efficient, involves checking that they have the maximum possible power to use the words they know. This means knowing which words have different grammatical uses, and identifying and being comfortable with the different word partnerships.

b.   Although the most common three word collocation system is verb-adjective-noun, the teacher should also note that verb-noun-noun combinations are quite common.

c.   Teachers may prefer to do this section by photocopying a page, asking students to underline experimentally, discuss the combinations the student has proposed, prepare personalised correct sentences, and then record the correct information in the student's personal copy of **Business English**. Clearly it is unwise to ask students to underline in coloured pens in their books for the permanent record, until you are sure that the information they are going to record is correct.

The final pages of this Section provide an opportunity for students to provide their own key words. This may be dealt with in a number of ways:

i.   The student provides a key word, the teacher photocopies the page and provides background words which the student then sorts in exactly the same way as the printed pages.

ii.   The student provides the key word and, working with business materials, a good dictionary etc provides his/her own background words and then proceeds as normal.

iii.   The student provides a background word and then, when working with resource texts, uses the page to record collocating words, together with their collocations and the usual personalised examples.

The teacher should note that the key word is always a noun, and if the teacher cannot immediately think of a small group of collocating words – say seven examples, the word is unlikely to prove fruitful for this kind of treatment. There are some words which are important, perhaps even essential, to the students' professional area which have a very limited collocational range. While these need to be learned during the course, they cannot provide the basis for a wide range of professional sentences in the same way that a key word can. **The key words in many ways provide an alternative to**

the grammatical syllabus for the professional student. By focusing on word-grammar rather than sentence grammar, they represent a real step towards the establishment of the lexical (word-based) syllabus discussed earlier in this Manual.

6.   BUSINESS GRAMMAR ORGANISER

As already discussed, one of the key compromises to be reached on in-service professional courses is that if students are doing a course which is too short for their real needs to be fulfilled, the most obvious price to be paid, among the many compromises which are necessary, is that grammatical accuracy must be sacrificed to communicative efficacy. At the same time most students already have considerable language learning experience, and most of that was probably in their state school system which valued grammar and grammatical accuracy highly. Once again, simply to ignore students' expectations and previous experience is unwise. For that reason **Business English** has a substantial section headed 'Business Grammar'. It must be said, however, that this section contains a wide variety of material, some of which teachers will not think of as specifically 'grammatical'.

Both students and teachers may be surprised that there is no formal grammar of the kind found in basic course books. There are three reasons for this:

a.   Most students doing in-service professional courses have already studied English, and most of the courses they have done will have emphasised grammar. Since the students are doing courses, they have presumably not benefitted fully from their previous learning. We have tried to avoid repeating that negative learning experience for the student. Instead we suggest new ways of approaching the language.

b.   We simply do not believe that grammar explanations and exercises are the most efficient way to improve the in-service professional student's ability to communicate more effectively in English.

c.   Through our testing of much of the material used in **Business English** it emerged that students' general level of vocabulary and grammar was not too bad. As we have already mentioned, it was their ability to put these together – their collocational power – which was lacking. Accordingly, we have constructed **Business English** largely to remedy that defect.

If teachers or students do want to do conventional grammar exercises, there are, of course, a large number of books providing these, directed both to professional and general English. It must be emphasised, however, that the insight offered in Section 5 into the communicative power of three word collocations makes clear that these collocations frequently provide the basic ungrammaticalised sentences of business English. However inelegant it may be, a student who says *'We receive order Germany'* will be understood. Grammaticalisation is always about expressing more subtle meanings. It is also important to remember that the average business person is considerably less interested in 'getting the language right' than language teachers frequently are (although we have all met students who are exceptions to this!). This provides an additional reason for the fact that **Business English** does not emphasise formal sentence grammar, and in particular the grammar of the verb ('tenses'). Far from being an oversight, it was a conscious and carefully researched choice which we made when preparing the material.

Broadly, this Section can be divided into six sections:

General Business Grammar (pp 78/83)

Grammar of Change (pp 84/95)

Word Families (pp 96/103)

'Reporting' verbs. (pp 104/107)

Expressions (pp 108/119)

Mistakes (pp 120/126)

General Business Grammar (78/83)

This short section suggests the **general** ways in which language can be made more diplomatic. Pages 78/80 show how there is a pattern for turning sentences such as *That's inconvenient* into the more diplomatic *Wouldn't it be a bit more convenient to* …. We suggest students should study Pages 78/80 as an introduction to this diplomatic language, but that, throughout any course, they should be constantly on the lookout for natural ways of expressing themselves. Suitable sources for this 'diplomatic language' are text book dialogues, audio or video recordings, and the language used in the lessons – it should not be too difficult for the teacher constantly to introduce useful language of this kind. Students should record a selection of expressions they think will be useful to them on Pages 81/83. This is another section where a major course objective is teaching the student to audit language (s)he hears for language worth recording in **Business English** for future productive use.

Grammar of Change (84/95)

The Grammar of Change section is the only part of the book which needs to be studied consecutively. The 12 pages are a single 'unit'and develop from introduction, to observation and practice, and finally to performance. The last two pages, Grammar of Change 11 and 12, could be used as the basis for a presentation, and integrated with the appropriate language from Sections 3 and 7 (Pages 130/131)

The central pages of this section are the nearest thing to conventional course book grammar. If teachers or students wish to have a lead from **Business English** to more formal study of the tenses, pages 86/87 provide the necessary link.

Because these 12 pages form the single most coherent grammar input in **Business English** we suggest that it will be appropriate on most courses which use the book for these pages to be a part of the course. They could be taught by a different teacher from the person handling the main course, or they could provide a thread running through from day to day or week to week. These pages will be most effective if they are studied as a complete unit.

Word Families (96/103)

This section is reminiscent of, and in some ways similar to, Section 5. While testing the material, as we have remarked elsewhere, we found many students knew one member of a word family but not the others. For relatively little extra learning load, the students' language ability could be significantly extended. This section, should, therefore be used when the student proposes a key word for the word partnership section which the teacher thinks has got an interesting family. The most important words are already included in the section, but, as usual, there is space for students to add their own words, and to produce personal and memorable examples.

Once again, the emphasis of **Business English** is on word grammar rather than sentence grammar. This section is what traditional grammar has called cognates, but here, following our usual policy of using simple terminology accessible to the student, we have preferred the term **Word Family**.

Reporting verbs (104/107)

This section will probably only appeal to students more interested in grammatical accuracy. During testing of the material it was discovered that many students frequently needed to report on earlier business conversations. Their vocabulary for doing this was frequently very defective – often being restricted to the verbs *say* and *tell*. Unfortunately, there is a wide range of verbs of this kind, though they behave grammatically in very different ways – some are followed by the infinitive, some by the ...*ing* form, some need an object etc. Teachers are warned that embarking on this section will require a certain amount of formal grammar! It is English for special purposes in a slightly different meaning of the word 'special' from that which is often used – English for those who definitely like to get the grammar right!

Expressions (108/119)

The pages of this section, covering 'have', two-word verbs, prepositions and prefixes, are very similar to many other pages of the book. The emphasis is on encouraging students to notice, record in writing, using natural examples, and record on tape, useful language which they are unlikely to have picked up from more conventional language courses. This means emphasis on multi-word phrases, two word verbs, and prepositional expressions. Obviously many of these can be done in two distinct ways:

a.   A page can be chosen and relatively formal grammar work done around it. For example, students can devote a lesson to collecting expressions using the empty verb *have* or they can deliberately audit professional materials for use for prepositional expressions with *by* etc.

b.   The students can be familiarised with these pages early in their course and then use them only from time to time, as expressions arise, to provide convenient recording formats. This method will be clearly preferred by teachers and students who want to de-emphasise grammar and are using **Business English** predominantly as a notebook and course record.

Mistakes (120/126)

The mistakes section is important for a number of reasons:

a.   It discusses the importance of mistakes, and emphasises to the students that not all mistakes are important. This comment was deliberately included to provide teachers with an opportunity to discuss this matter with students, and to support the teachers in emphasising the distinction between effective and defective English.

We suggest that for most students it will be appropriate to discuss the comment at the top of page 120 early in the course, ideally on Day 1.

b.   Having established that not all mistakes are important, we have deliberately provided a very restricted space for students to record 'Important Mistakes'. There is surely a lack of proportion on the part of the teacher or student if they feel the need to record too many mistakes as 'Important'. The restricted number of pages provided for this purpose is intended subconsciously to suggest to the student that only a few mistakes actually fall into this category.

c.   The two example mistakes are deliberately very different. The first is an irritating slip – perhaps something the student wants to record because (s)he is aware of it as something (s)he frequently gets wrong. The second mistake is not a wrong detail; instead, the whole sentence is misconceived and needs to be re-thought in English. It is given so that teachers may exploit it to draw students' attention to this kind of mistake, so that they may look for others during their course and record the full natural sentence, rather than working only on tiny details.

d.   The Word Contrast pages are, on the whole, intended for students at lower levels of ability and to highlight for them frequent confusions. As usual, there is ample space for students and teachers to decide to record confusions peculiar to that particular student. Many of these mistakes tend to be false friends, and so differ according to the student's native language. For this reason we have provided only a few examples and left plenty of space for student and teacher input.

Summary

It is important to realise that Section 6 contains a fairly wide range of different types of material. It is also the section where the level of the different pages is most marked. We imagine that in a typical course, teachers and students will want to **select** from this Section. It would be an oddly balanced course, and not one we would recommend, if students completed all the pages in this Section!

7.   PROFESSIONAL LANGUAGE ORGANISER

As we have already discussed, modern theory suggests that native speakers have access to a much larger range of learned sentences than language teachers usually think. This suggests that students, too, may need to learn a repertoire of professional gambits. It is important to realise that language of this type:

– can be learned by heart, and reproduced.
– is no use unless you also have something to say!

Giving a presentation (127/131)

We cannot emphasise too strongly the importance we attach to this section. We believe that any professional course will be more effective if the students are aware from early in the course that there is to be a product, which is to be produced by a fixed time. For most students, the most likely product is a spoken presentation, with accompanying visuals etc. which they will 'perform' towards the end of their course (there may be more than one if the course is of a more-extended kind). The stereotyped language presented on Pages 130/131 is only a small part of the input that will be required for an effective presentation. In addition, students should be using pages from the **Word Partnership** section, the **Resource Text** section, and elements of **Social Language** which will be useful for a presentation.

Suitable topics for the presentation could include:
The student's company.
A particular product.
Aspect of the student's company/country (see pp 94/95).

On some much less business orientated courses, a topic the student is interested in, a presentation of the student's home town etc.

A more comprehensive list of possible topics for a student presentation is provided elsewhere in this Teachers' Manual (see pp 52/3).

If students do perform an oral presentation towards the end of their course, we strongly recommend that, if possible, this is recorded. The student should be given a copy of the recording, so that when (s)he returns and the training manager asks what was achieved on the course, rather than attempting to describe the course, a student can simply present the training manager with real evidence of linguistic achievement in a professional area.

Telephone language (132/3)

There are books on the market which claim to teach 'telephone English' but the fact is that apart from a few fixed phrases – gambits – what we say on the telephone is remarkably similar to what we say in face-to-face situations; it is the **content** we wish to express, rather than the gambits, which is of primary importance. At the same time, the gambits are important, precisely because so much of this language is stereotyped. Listeners, particularly native speakers, **expect** to hear particular phrases, and if they hear only one or two words, will supply the rest themselves. For this reason, it is important that the gambits are learned exactly, and spoken with good stress and intonation. Unfortunately, we are very aware that we are suggesting that students learn language by heart. Obviously, this language is most likely to be remembered if the teacher devises supplementary activities which will activate and reinforce the language as printed in the book. With small groups it may well be appropriate to organise meetings at which both the teacher and individual students take the chair (see page 7). With **all** students, and particularly one-to-one, it is important that they have a chance to practise telephone language **actually on the telephone**.

Project approach (see Teachers' Manual, page 17)

For students who are on a course in an English-speaking country, we strongly suggest that some kind of project be agreed between the student, teacher and institution providing the course. This could result in the student arranging or confirming his/her visit to a local company, travel or hotel arrangements etc. The more authentic this project is, the more likely it is to engage the student and to provide focus and purpose for any more formal classroom practice of this stereotyped language.

Professional Meetings (136/7)

We have already proposed (see BE Page 7) that some lessons be constructed following a meeting format. If this is done, the stereotyped language provided on these pages could be photocopied and provided for the students so that they may keep it in front of them throughout those lessons/meetings.

Once again we would urge teachers not to underestimate the importance of asking students to repeat aloud some of this language several times until students feel comfortable with it. Again, it may be appropriate to ask them to record some of this language on their cassette tapes.

Important Verbs (138/146)

Good dictionaries of business English such as the Longman Dictionary of Business English are useful resources. Observation of such dictionaries will, however, show up a rather curious feature of them – they are filled with nominal collocations – in simple English they are full of nouns. As we have already indicated in the Introduction, and in discussing Section 5, the students' communicative effectiveness is frequently impaired because of their lack of collocational power – they do not know the verbs which go with their key nouns. Clearly, then, teachers and students require access to a list of verbs used in business English. The list provided on pages 144/146 is based on extensive observation of business English language teaching course books, company literature, and well known business publications such as The Financial Times, The Economist, The International Herald Tribune etc. The list contains about 500 verbs which are frequent in such texts. This number indicates the size of the task facing many low level business students – their total vocabulary may be only 1500 words, and yet they appear to need as many as 500 verbs to read 'ordinary' business English text.

The primary purpose of this list is to help teachers who, in turn, should pass on this necessary auditing skill to the students during their course. If the student can identify a Key noun (See Pages 58/9) the teacher can use the verb check list to test which of the verbs form frequent word partnerships with the key word.

Things you can do with the list of important business verbs (144/146)

Ask the student to choose a letter and look at the verbs which begin with it. Then ask him or her to:

— Find all the verbs which are **also** nouns.

— Make nouns from the other verbs (**divide/division**).

— Think of a suitable partner word or words to follow each verb (**apply for a job, appoint a new director**).

— Use a dictionary to translate new verbs.

— Find the equivalents for L1 verbs called out by the teacher.

— Match the verbs with a list of partner words prepared by the teacher.

— Make sentences, questions, suggestions etc, from each verb or the word partnerships created from it.

— Think of suitable verbs to go before the noun-forms of each verb (**consult, consultancy, provide consultancy**).

— Make tables from a set of verbs, all of which collocate with a given **set** of nouns. (**accept, adjust, agree ... the offer/terms/arrangements**).

— Divide the verbs into groups according to number of syllables, and syllable stress.

— Find all the verbs containing a particular phoneme.

— Find all the verbs containing a particular letter or letters (eg 'o') and distinguish different pronunciations of same letter in different words.

— Find opposites for each verb.

— Find synonyms and contrast the word partnerships that can be formed from them.

— Use the verbs as the basis of gap-filling, dictation or listening exercises based on the ideas above.

— Identify the irregular verbs and their past tense and participle.

— Make a set of cards with a verb on one side and partner words/noun-forms/gapped sentences on the other.

— Match each verb with a suitable partner word or words (**apply, apply for, apply for a job**).

— Find all the verbs which match a given Keyword (**address, ask for, arrange ... a meeting**).

— Guess the Keyword going with a set of verbs (**delay, deliver, dispatch** ... an order).

— Identify the prepositions, if any, which can or must follow a given verb, giving an example sentence in each case.

— Identify verbs requiring a following gerund/infinitive.

— Identify verbs that can be followed by (a) a WH-word (**agree how to** ...), (b) a **that** clause (**he argued that** ...), or (c) an indirect object (**ask him a question**).

Notice these are all examples of grammar teaching, but **word grammar**, rather than the more traditional sentence grammar.

8. CULTURAL BACKGROUND ORGANISER

Language is part of our behaviour, and using English as a foreign language brings with it a range of problems which many students do not foresee. There are two broadly different categories – non-native speakers using English among themselves, and non-native speakers using English to native speakers of the language. Ironically, for students whose general level of language ability is low, the problems are relatively few – if they make 'social' mistakes, these will usually be put down to their poor level of English. On the other hand, if students' general level of English is good, it is often assumed by native speakers to be very good or even fluent – in other words they make little or no allowance for the fact that the competent foreign speaker is both using a foreign language, and operating with a different set of cultural assumptions. Cross-cultural communication is a complex topic, and is rapidly emerging as a discipline in its own right. It is unrealistic to expect a relatively short in-service ESP course to provide the necessary details of how to do business in the Middle East or Japan. We thought it important, however, that students should at least be made aware of their own ethnocentricity – What **I** think is normal, **is** normal!

These pages are intended:

a. To make the student more aware of the fact that cultural assumptions may differ greatly from country to country. The signs which we think we can read, may mislead us considerably. It is perhaps worth reminding teachers that many of them, having taught different nationalities over quite a long period, may be much more aware of cultural difference than language students who may have only done business in their own country, or possibly with one other country.

b. The material should provide teachers and students with an opportunity for more informal discussions. Many business English courses, in an effort to be 'serious', can become rather monochrome, concentrating heavily on business texts and professional language. This section is intended to be a serious element in a balanced business course, but also to provide an opportunity for more relaxed conversation between students and teacher.

In most cases this section is likely to be most useful if students complete the Questionnaires individually, either outside class, or before any discussion. Discussion should ensue, particularly in mixed nationality groups, but also when students of the same cultural background are unable to agree.

Teachers' attitude

It is extremely important that teachers avoid taking a judgmental position. The teacher's role is constantly to remind students that 'Ah, so **you** do it like that, but other people do it differently'. The single key word that teachers must keep in the forefront of their minds when handling this section is that people do things **differently** in different parts of the world. If these pages have a 'message' it should only be to encourage curiosity and tolerance. We hope very strongly that at no point will the teacher suggest to students how anyone **should** behave. However strong your own views are on some of the issues raised, it is important for you, too, to recognise your own ethnocentricity!

In general, each page of this section is independent of the others, although as already indicated, the overall feel is to encourage an **appreciation of difference.** We suggest that it may be appropriate to do one of the topics in this section each day of a one- or two-week intensive course, or each week of a longer-term course. We sincerely hope that nobody will contemplate working through the section page by page.

The Case Study (pages 156/8) needs to be handled with particular sensitivity. It contains one key piece of information, derived from research in the field of cross-cultural communication – all of us have stereotypes in our head, and stereotypes are **always, essentially negative**. The person who describes the German or Japanese as 'hard working', never means it as a compliment! Judgements which might, elsewhere, be regarded positively, are to be interpreted negatively when attributed to stereotypic figures. We **all** have these prejudices, and effective business communication is helped if we are aware of them, and can lower the opposition which some cultural misunderstanding can create. Presenting this idea to some students requires tact and diplomacy.

10. NOTES ON PARTICULAR PAGES

In general, we believe teachers familiar with the field of business English will want to adapt material for particular courses and particular students in a wide variety of ways. We have, therefore, given only general notes on the kind of material contained in each section. We assumed teachers who enjoyed using this material would feel restricted rather than helped by the kind of line-by-line notes sometimes given with general course books. We do believe, however, that teachers might be helped by comments on a few individual pages. Here are those notes.

Page 7. Worth using early in the course, particularly with small groups where the 'lessons as meetings' idea will be most effective.

Page 13. If students know the words at the bottom of the page they should have no difficulty recycling them into the 'diary pages'; if they do not know them, they will almost certainly be useful vocabulary and are worth teaching. Don't forget, that, as with a lot of this input language, it may be necessary to do pronunciation practice, or ask students to put the language in sentences at a later stage in the course.

Pages 14/15. Experience shows that students often have language needs which they do not realise themselves, particularly when they use English in particular situations which occur only infrequently. These pages are intended to provide a framework to help the students think more clearly about the situations they find themselves in throughout the year. We suggest you might want to refer to this **at least twice** during the course, to see if students want to add anything after they have settled down into a routine on the course.

Page 16. This page provides an early introduction to the concept of Word Partnerships, which are also developed on Pages 57/59 and 138/139. We have deliberately provided three different entry points to this key idea which lies behind much of the syllabus design of **Business English**.

Pages 21/21. After they have been completed neatly, these pages could be copied on to overhead transparency and used as part of the student presentation of his/her company.

Page 24/26. More lighthearted; suitable for conversations but still providing useful personal language.

Page 28. Do not ignore this even with quite competent speakers! Draw particular attention to the two words at the bottom of the page, and provide a lead to Page 34, which is difficult for all students and of more importance than they tend to believe.

Page 29. Emphasise the importance of *I'm afraid*. Many students feel uncomfortable using this expression because they associate it with *I'm afraid of the dark*. Use it frequently yourself, highlight it, and then encourage them to feel natural using an important, but unusual English expression. This is of less importance if students are predominantly going to use their English with other non-native speakers.

Page 35. Very useful for lower level students for early in the course. For some students, whose language level is very low, you may like to photocopy this page so they can keep it in front of them all the time.

Page 40. As suggested elsewhere, students should practise these regularly. They should also practise delivering them to a fairly large room at adequate volume.

Pages 45 to 76. These are fully discussed in this Manual under the Section 4 and Section 5 headings.

Pages 78/80 and 81/83. These pages are partly about language, and partly about social behaviour – being diplomatic or tactful. Expect a different reaction from different nationalities. With some students you may think they do not need to produce this language, but they should at least recognise it if it is used to them. This material should not be taught without adequate discussion with the students; no attempt should be made to 'teach the student to be British'. It could be helpful to link this section to Section 8, as this language use is, to some extent, a cultural feature.

Pages 86/95. Discussed elsewhere in this Manual (Page 32).

Pages 104/107. These pages cross-refer to Pages 122/123.

Page 124/126. Mostly useful for lower level students. Encourage students to record two interesting and memorable example sentences. Again there is a notional two column format for allowing checking of recall by masking the right-hand column.

Page 127. A useful grammatical page for low level students who over-use the words *possible* and *necessary*. Probably best to approach this page as a result of student errors.

Page 128. Possible 'link' page, if you wish to do more formal grammar. Rather than naming the tenses in the traditional way, we propose more 'business-like' name, e.g. *accomplishments* for present perfect. Again a page more useful for students of lower level.

Page 138/143. These provide another way of approaching the word partnerships. They could be used as revision for the material presented in the book on Pages 60/76.

It cannot be emphasised too strongly that there is no 'right' way of using particular pages of **Business English**. The whole purpose is to provide a flexible and open approach. We hope teachers will use it in this spirit.

11. PREPARATORY ACTIVITIES

There are a number of types of preparatory activity that can be used to work **around** and **towards** the content of any given page or section of the book. These have the advantage that when students then come to fill in, or work from, these pages, they already know what they are doing. The use of the book, then, takes a central place in between preparatory and follow-up activities, and serves its purpose in providing a clean and practised record of language work done in advance **around** its material.

Any or all of the activities suggested may be used in any sequence. Where particular activities are strongly appropriate to particular pages or sections, this is indicated.

1. Brainstorming.

This is particularly useful with the following sections: **Needs, Keywords, Eating Out, Grammar of Change, Telephone Language, Business Prepositions, Word Lobsters**.

Brainstorming serves the obvious purpose of eliciting vocabulary and determining what the student(s) know(s) already.

Elicitation can be done from the class as a whole, by students working in pairs or small groups, coming one by one to write on the board.

2. Presentations

These are also a way of gauging what student(s) can already do and what language they lack, and can be oriented around particular pages or sections, for example pages of the **Language Learning Organiser,** the **Personal Language Organiser,** or **Grammar of Change** (see pages 94/5).

As students speak, the teacher silently writes on the board appropriate words, word partnerships, and phrases that are missing from the student's language, tying these in with language in the book so that the latter will provide reinforcement when it is used.

Students can be asked to reformulate each others' presentations (in the 1st or 3rd person) using the new language written up by the teacher.

3. Dictation

This is an excellent way of pre-familiarising the student(s) with language in the book. It can be done by the teacher simply reading and the students writing individually, or by getting the student(s) to immediately re-dictate to the teacher what they have heard, with the student using silence to elicit self-correction.

If the students write what they hear individually, they can be asked to compare their transcriptions in pairs, and produce an agreed version. One member from each pair then works with a representative of another pair to agree a version, and so on until the whole class sends a representative to write up a final version on board. This would work well with, for example dictating the sentence heads in the **Personal Language Organiser**. Students write what they hear **and** complete the sentences as they write.

4. Listening – dictation and sorting practice

Dictation can be used with all the pages of the book containing any sort of language input. It becomes particularly valuable when designed as a sorting exercise, and can be used with **Keywords, General Business Grammar** or **Social Language**.

a. Teacher dictates a mixed set of verbs and adjectives around a keyword and the students sort them into two groups .... and then guess the keyword.

b. Teacher dictates a mixed set of words, some of which form partnerships with one keyword, the others with another. Students write them in two columns according to which keyword they collocate with.

c. Teacher dictates a mixed set of words some of which come before and some after, a particular keyword.

d. Teacher dictates a mixed set of utterances, some diplomatic (see pp 81/83) and others crude. The students sort them into two groups and look at the contrasts.

e. Teacher dictates a mixed set of time expressions, verbs of increase and decrease, phrases with two different functional heads (see page 41) and the students **identify** the groups to which expressions belong.

5. Insistence questions

The principle here is to repeat the same question over and over again, so that the person responding must provide an ever-expanding range and variety of answers. Insistence questions can be used not only to practise but also to generate a lexical database, by exposing the student to the blind spots in his/her vocabulary. Here is an example:

The teacher prepares a detailed job description in collocational form: *handle* the *mail, file documents, service* the *telephone, prepare meetings*. The student(s) repeatedly asks the **same** question '*What do you do?* each time receiving a **different** answer. Having heard and listed the tasks the student(s) may put another insistence question: *What does ... involve?* They then receive a breakdown of this task, once again in collocational form: *taking calls, putting people through, taking messages* etc. Alternatively they may be given a detailed task list in answer to the first question, and then be asked to sort and group the tasks under different headings themselves.

This exercise provides a model of needs analysis. The student(s) are then put into the position of having to answer the insistence questions and come up with language defining their own jobs, in this form. This will expose their language needs, allowing the teacher the opportunity to feed in language whenever necessary. Alternatively the students can conduct the insistence interview in pairs, with the trainees writing down in their mother tongue anything they are not able to express in English.

What are you doing? The teacher again gives a range of answers, of things he or she is currently engaged in, though not necessarily at the moment of speaking. It would be useful to begin with those activities of shortest duration and end with activities that have been ongoing for months or possibly years, but for which the . . .*ing* form is still used to indicate their temporary character in the mind of the speaker. The tables are then turned and the student(s) give answers:

I am sitting in a chair, I am doing a course, I am learning English, I am doing a research project for my company etc.

The main focus is the collocational language around which the particular structures and verb forms are practised.

Insistence questions can be done with one student answering many times successively, or as an 'answer and pass on the question' activity, going round the group several times.

Many pages of the book can be worked around in this way particularly the opening sections of the book (**Language Learning Organiser** and **Personal Language Organiser**, and also page 128.

6. Dialogue building

The teacher dictates one or more functional expressions, sentence heads, or word partnerships from a page in the book, and the students visualise a situation and build a three- or five-line dialogue around it.

This can be a pairwork activity, with the teacher first hearing and reformulating each pair's dialogue, and pairs then role-playing the other pairs' dialogues.

7. Dictionary work

Some sections of the book ask the students to use their dictionaries as a resource in checking the meaning or usage of particular words, or to gather examples of word partnerships. (for example **Business Verbs** page 104/7).

This is best done as a pair or small group activity. Students can also be asked to brainstorm in L1 and then use dictionaries to gather vocabulary. It is important to have available good mono- and bi-lingual dictionaries of business English.

8. Translation work

Some pages of the book ask the students to write equivalents of certain expressions in their own language. These can be brainstormed first, or the expressions divided among different students for translation into L1 and then swopped for re-translation into English. Varieties of translation can be elicited and discussed, or translations prepared by discussion in groups.

9. Cards

Used as a preparatory activity, the teacher prepares sets of cards in one, two or three colours, for the students to work with by sorting, matching, sequencing, or translating the words or phrases written on them, for example:

a. A set of cards in two colours for creating word partnerships by matching one card from one colour set with its partner from the other colour set.

This can be turned into a game of Snap, in which each partner has one colour set, and the first to call out the word "partnership" wins the two cards when a card from one set matches the last card played.

b. "Happy Families" can be played with cards based on Word Families, page 96.

Such games can be made more challenging by requiring the students to make sentences from the words or phrases on the cards they play or win.

10. Overhead projector

a. Prepare transparencies of pages you intend to work with, and do oral work around them **before** the students turn to their books and write in them.

b. Get students to prepare transparencies from pages of the book that they have filled in and make presentations from them as a follow-up activity.

12. FOLLOW UP ACTIVITIES

Most of the Preparatory Activities can also be used as follow-up work, with the balance and choice to be decided by the teacher. In addition there are two activities that lend themselves specifically to follow-up work:

1. Recording

Particularly appropriate and useful to one-to-one work, or as a homework activity if Walkmans are available.

The student(s) can be asked to record language written into, or contained in their books, along with translations in their own language. Different patterns of recording may be used, for example **L2-pause-L1-pause-L2-pause.** On replaying their cassettes the students can stop the tape at regular intervals and do one of several things:

– Translate mentally.

– Repeat mentally.

– Anticipate the next word (either a partner word or a translation).

– Make a sentence/question from the word.

– Recall the previous item or anticipate the next.

– Transcribe and then check with their books.

– Practise saying the word in different ways.

2. Drills

These can be extremely effective for both memorising, activating, and deploying the word partnerships in a *communicative way*. In using these drills we recommend that the students face each other on opposite sides of a desk, or, in one-to-one, that the teacher changes position so as to be sitting opposite the student. Eye-contact should be encouraged when either partner is speaking.

a. Acknowledgement Drill

The "coach" (either teacher or S1) reads each partnership in the list several times. The "trainee" student simply listens, allowing the repetition to continue until he or she feels that the words have really "sunk in". If they wish they may echo them silently by mouthing, but there is no requirement to memorise but simply to absorb both meaning and sound. When the trainee feels it is time to go on to the next partnership on the list, he or she gives a verbal sign of acknowledgement, such as *I see, Go on, Right*. A sample of these verbal signals should be provided on the board.

When the list has been gone through by two students, "trainee" and "coach" reverse roles. If the teacher is taking the role of "coach" he or she should repeat each item in a different manner each time (using the words in sentences, varying tone of voice etc.)

b. Dynamic drills

Here the Trainee student has the list of word-partnership vocabulary in front of him or her, but the Coach is armed with another list ... of different ways in which the trainee can **Say it** for example:

softly	**as a question**	**while getting up**
rapidly	**as an order**	**while sitting down**
loudly	**as if you were feeling ill**	**with surprise**
angrily	**as if you were doubtful**	**with pleasure**
seriously	**to yourself**	**with alarm**
slowly	**to a child**	**with a smile**
mysteriously	**to a large audience**	**with a gesture**

The Trainee reads each item on his or her list in the manner instructed by the Coach. Every item is given a different **Say it** instruction by the Coach. If the Coach is not satisfied that the Trainee has really used the manner instructed, the instruction may be repeated. The Coach may also actively **model** the manner in which he or she is instructing the Trainee to speak. For example, if the Coach says *Say it angrily*, the word *angrily* should be said angrily.

You will find that Coach and Trainee have great fun combining instructions. For example *Say it with a laugh while getting up* or *Say it slowly as if dreaming*.

You will also find that the students who are coaching can't wait to become the Trainees and have a go at dramatic speaking themselves ... taking the spotlight.

c. Activation drills

Here the Trainee student is invited to make a sentence from each word partnership on the list. The instruction can be more specific ie make a question, make a request, make a suggestion etc. If the teacher is acting as Coach, he or she may wish to provide help to the student, or do additional work (reformulation, drills) around particularly meaningful and professionally relevant utterances that the student constructs.

If the drill is conducted in parallel by several pairs of students, the students acting as Coach should be basically passive, and instructed to "pass" the Trainee's sentence if they find it both meaningful and free of any gross errors that they can identify. Alternatively, they can be instructed to give a meaningful response (acknowledgement or answer) to each utterance that the Trainee produces.

Afterwards, both Trainee and Coach may, before changing roles, be asked to write down at least 5 sentences that they can remember from the drill. These can then become the basis of groupwork and reformulation.

d. Testing drills

There are many varieties of drills that can be practised in which one or both students test each other in recalling partner words. Either or both students may have before them a word-partnership list in which one column is masked. If the students are

47

testing each other they should each mask the column which is unmasked for their partner. They can then either go through the list sequentially (mutual testing) or pick cue words at random from the list (with one student being the Coach and having both columns visible).

They can score each other on points for successful recall. This is a useful revision drill, and like all the drills, can be done by pairs of students out of class as well as in class.

e. Group drills

The principle of the group drill is that the students themselves **are** words. For example, they are each whispered or given a word on a card, and then, on command must go to one or other side of the classroom: nouns on one side, adjectives on the other. Having thus divided into two groups, the adjectives must then find a suitable partner-noun. The students then have acted out a basic sort and match exercise with a set of word partnerships.

This can be done with adjectives and nouns, nouns and verbs, singulars and plurals, words that come before and after a keyword such as *sales*: sales **manager, appoint** a sales **manager**), positive and negative auxiliaries: in fact any binary lexical or synatactic contrast.

Alternatively, each student can be given a keyword. The students take it in turns to stand in the centre of a circle. If the keyword (eg "sales") is standing at the centre, the students in the circle must each call out a different word partnership involving the keyword (*sales force, sales network* etc). After one round another student and another keyword take the centre.

The students here act out collocational fields around a keyword. Group drills can also be used to practise sentence building from word partnerships. Here, each student is allocated a particular 'part of speech' (adjective, verb, question word, auxiliary verb, main verb, noun etc).

A noun is asked to volunteer an example word. Other students then come forward to volunteer partners and form a human sentence chain from the starting word.

Alternatively the students can be asked to form groups, each of which contains all the necessary parts of speech for a sentence. Each group then arranges itself in a human sentence chain, and, constructs example sentences. The words of the sentences may be spoken one at a time, with each student providing his or her component part of speech. Afterwards the students may be asked to each utter or think up a complete sentence. Finally the students write down what they have produced. The students act, in this way, as a sort of group mind and group voice, arranging and rearranging sentence patterns. If they are standing in a line this can be made into a quick-change drill in which the student at the end of the sentence moves to the front position and starts a new sentence.

f. Instruction drills

Here the students enact, give and/or prepare series of physical instructions. These can be used to practise a wide variety of verb-noun and prepositional collocations.

Body exercises: raise your arms, bend your knees, touch your forehead. Realia exercises: pick up your pen, write down a word, open your book, pass the book to your neighbour etc.

Prepositional keywords: Look out of the window, look for a dictionary, look up a word, look at the person next to you etc.

Operating instructions: plug in the recorder, press eject, insert a cassette, close the flap etc.

Mime exercises: unlock the door, get into the car, fasten your seat belt, insert your key, turn on the ignition etc.

Visualisation exercises: Imagine you are standing by your front door. Unlock it. Go inside. Go into your living room. Look around. Is it dark or light? If dark, switch on a light etc.

g. More mental drills

These are things for students to do **silently** on hearing a lexical item read out. Like those for the dynamic drill, various instructions can be given around any one item.

let it echo in your mind
get an image of the words
hear/see yourself saying it to someone
think the meaning
think of another word to go with it
give it a colour
put it somewhere in the room

The instructions are given before the item is read out. Students may like to have their eyes closed for many of them.

h. Ball drills

Ball drills can be used to practise collocations and stuctures in an almost endless number of ways, with the powerful advantage that the drills are conducted standing up, and combine movement and speech. In other words they are fun, providing a "get up and do it" element, and can be used successfully in both group and one-to-one work.

The basic rule is "speak and throw", changing or adding to the cue phrase in a way modelled by the teacher. Here are a number of alternatives:

i. First word drills

Teacher throws the ball up in the air three times, each time changing the first word: *will you, do you, can you*. Then throws the ball to the first student to pass on, adding more variations as the ball goes round the class. If a student gets stuck the ball is returned to the teacher, who may provide a prompt, correct a mistake, end the drill, or change the drill into a new one. If the teacher raises a hand this should be a signal for the ball to be returned allowing the teacher to end or change the drill: *have you, did you*... return to teacher... *did she* ... on to students... *will she, can she* etc. More examples of first word drills:

Personnel Manager, Training Manager, Sales Manager etc. *attend a meeting, arrange a meeting, postpone a meeting* etc. *fixed costs, variable costs, direct costs* etc. *will reach the target, might reach the target, can reach the target*

ii. Last word drills

have breakfast, have a break, have a talk, have a drink (see page 108/9) *afraid I can't, afraid I haven't, afraid I won't* (see page 29) *sales area, sales figures, sale manager* (see page 61).

iii. Add a-word-drills

sales,
sales manager,
appoint a sales manager,
appoint a new sales manager,
we need to appoint a new sales manager,
we need to appoint a new sales manager for Germany,
we need to appoint a new sales manager for Germany soon,
etc.

iv. Structure drills:

The elements in this drill are not words but phrases or words classes, for example *time-subject-trend figures* (see page 84)

In April-productivity-improved-by 2%
In June-stock-increased-by 5%

A new word or phrase is provided for **each** element of the structure, so that a string of sentences is produced. A variant on this is to divide the class into as many groups as there are elements, with the ball being passed from group to group. Alternatively, four individuals can be chosen to stand in line. When the ball reaches the end of the sentence it is passed back to the person in front. If one student gets stuck, another may take his or her place in the sentence structure.

v. Sentence head drills:

The ball is passed and each student completes the same sentence eg *I am responsible for...*, *What I like about my job is* ..., etc (see pp 18/25, 41/44, 130/131).

13. SUPPLEMENTARY LISTS OF SUGGESTIONS

On the following pages you will find a range of lists taken over directly from Peter Wilberg's *One to One, A Teachers' Handbook* published by LTP (ISBN 0 906717 61 2). In a few cases the lists use terminology introduced and discussed in the earlier book, which was written before the approach and sophisticated formats of **Business English** were devised. We are confident, however, that these lists provide any teacher of business English with a wide range of possibilities in a quickly accessible form.

If you are new to teaching business people in one-to-one or small group situations, or have experienced frustration in this area of teaching, think about the suggestions on page 56; if you feel your small group lessons are cluttered, use pages 58/9.

While the suggestions in this section were not written to integrate directly with the material and approach of **Business English**, they provide complementary activities and suggestions which we are sure many readers will find helpful.

Possible topics for a student presentation

Company organisation and subsidiaries
　　　　history
　　　　growth
　　　　policy
Marketing strategy
Product range
　　　　descriptions
New products
Best-selling products
Product development

Further techniques and options

Market share

Results and projections

Personal career history
Career objectives
Position and contribution to company

Sales organisation
　　　strategy, training
Market trends
Managerial style

Negotiations in hand
Future negotiations

Reports (eg past year)

Describing colleagues (introductions and profiles)

The competition
The customers

Timetable for next month

Economic and political climate in home country
Environmental issues
Teach the teacher your job: responsibilities
　　　　　　　　　　product information
　　　　　　　　　　people information
　　　　　　　　　　briefing for negotiations
　　　　　　　　　　advice

Advertising

Suggested topics for biographical talks

My best learning experience
My first job
My last job
My secret ambition
My best friend
My worst accident
My worst illness
My greatest regret
My proudest achievement
My hopes for the next 5 years
My greatest disappointment
My strongest belief
My most important decision
My job and what I like about it
My city/town/village and what I
like about it
My country and what I like about it
My closest call with death
My biggest business risk
My biggest inspiration
My most memorable dream

The worst job I ever had
The most important lesson life has
taught me
The longest minute I ever spent
The best year of my life
The strangest person I ever met
The most interesting person I ever
met
The most courageous act I ever
witnessed
The biggest crisis of my life
The person I admire most
The greatest help I ever received
The thing that interests me most in
people
The strangest coincidence in my
life

How I have changed
How I reached my present
position
How my company started
How I overcame a habit
How I overcame a weakness
How I overcame a fear
How one idea increased my
happiness

The last time I had a flat tyre

The last time I fell in love
The last time I felt envy
The last time I got angry
The last time I got drunk
The last time I spoke English
(before this course)
The last time I was in pain
The last time I remembered a dream
The last time I was terrified

Why I am not religious
Why I am not an atheist
Why I smoke
Why I vote the way I do

If I lived again . . .
If I had a past life . . .
If I had the chance . . .
If I had the courage . . .
If I had the power . . .
If I had the skill . . .

The three most vivid scenes I
recall from my life
The three most important people
in my life
The three most important men/
women in my life
The three most important
principles I follow
The three most important qualities
for someone in my position

A secret I am prepared to reveal
about myself
A book that influenced me for life
A person that influenced me for
life
An event that influenced me for life

A place I would love to visit again
A person I would love to meet
again
An era I would like to have lived in

Something I will never do again
Something I often dream about

What I hope my children will learn
from me
What I do with the most confidence
What I hope to achieve this year

Things to look for in your interaction with the student

With all **your** beliefs and ideas in mind, here is a check list of how it can affect your interaction in the classroom.

- Are you forcing the pace or lagging behind your student's drive?
- Is your student 'performing' mechanically or with real motivation?
- Are you confident of the 'how' and 'why' of what you are doing and is this confidence shared by your student?
- Are you over-controlling communication or allowing your student to dominate?
- Are you sharing decisions with your student or taking all responsibility on yourself?
- Are you giving your student options, dictating or negotiating the work you do?
- Are you adapting to your student's conversational and working style?
- Is your assessment of your student's motivation accurate or are you guiding yourself and your student by false projections or assumptions?
- Does your student know his or her own motivation clearly and can you help him or her to clarify objectives?
- Do you push on regardless with an activity despite negative signals of boredom, tiredness or dissatisfaction from your student?
- Do you take steps to obtain explicit feedback from your student?
- Do you provide feedback to your student when you realise he or she has a problem?
- Are you on the look-out for topics or activities that the student responds positively to and do you build on these?
- Do you allow work to proceed haphazardly or do you review and re-clarify course objectives whenever necessary?
- Are you aware of your own areas of ignorance, admit and take steps to compensate for these?
- Are there feelings you don't allow yourself in teaching? How much do you restrict or facilitate your own personality and self-expression?
- Do you give your student opportunities to teach you?
- Do you think about what this particular student's manner and personality is teaching you?
- Do you allow yourself to learn from your student?
- Do you give yourself time to recollect your observations and feelings after each working period?
- Do you allow yourself and your student 'off-'days or periods?
- Do you permit yourself breathing space, freedom of movement and sufficient breaks?
- Do you give your student opportunities for work alone without fussing and interfering?

Things you can do before day 1

- Find out your student's name, age and suposed level
- Find out your student's job and nationality
- Obtain a copy of his or her application/registration form
- Obtain any professional material that your student can or has supplied
- Obtain any test material completed by your student
- Conduct a prior interview if possible
- Speak to anyone who knows or has spoken to the student if possible
- Obtain any file that may exist on the student, or on his or her company, or speciality
- Audit the above information—see p. 22
- Audit the student's L1 if this is unfamilair to you
- Audit any coursebook or other material that may be relevant to this student's needs

In this context auditing means examining with particular emphasis on the implications for language *form*. What kind of lexis is likely to be appropriate for the student? What kind of *specific* situation is (s)he likely to face? What kind of interference mistakes are likely, bearing in mind the student's L1?

It is never possible to predict in advance what an individual one-to-one student will need; as we have already said the chief skill is the teacher's response-ability. At the same time, part of the teacher's general responsibility is to examine all materials which are available in advance critically from a language point of view, in order to ensure maximum possible advance preparation for the student's needs.

- Gather authentic material that may be useful (eg if you are teaching an optician, visit an opticians)
- Use public libraries for specialised reference sources
- Check the available language teaching literature for special purpose texts
- Ensure the availability of any dictionaries, general or specialised, mono- and bi-lingual that may be required
- Ensure the availability of any equipment that you may wish to use
- Collate, design, copy or reformat material you may require on day 1
- Check the room you will be using for ventilation, adequate seating and desk space, room for equipment, electrical sockets, lighting and heating, noise etc.
- Obtain or put in requests for additional items of furniture, decor, equipment, or conveniences
- Decide on a seating arrangement
- Make all copies in good time
- Make necessary enquiries regarding any visits you could arrange for your student

Suggestions for creating space for learning

- Make sure your table/desk top does not take away space for 'get up and do it' activities. Move it near a window if possible.

- Decide if you will sit opposite or at right angles to your student. Some students prefer the latter, and this may be necessary if you are sharing books or studying materials.

- If the room is bare or drab bring something to liven it up: posters, pictures and plants. Wall charts (home-made or commercial) can also be very useful.

- If you have a larger space available or are working in a living room plan your use of space accordingly: make use of armchairs to create a more relaxed atmosphere or for passive listening.

- Plan for breaks at more or less regular intervals: not only the twice daily coffee break, but more frequent and briefer pauses for a quick 'get up and stretch' routine.

- Make sure there is a white/blackboard available. If there is not, make a fuss about it. This is *essential* equipment not only for clear presentation but to create a sense of space by allowing both teacher and student to 'get up and write' and by providing a *focus* in space.

- Occasionally swop seats or alter seating positions (for example during a writing exercise or when the student is using the board). As well as providing a change this can have symbolic value (student as teacher!)

- Adopt the attitude right at the start that *you can't do everything* in a short course. You'll feel better as a result and it will allow you to really *give time* to your student. More real progress will be achieved this way.

- Make full use of silence, gesture and pausing in your own speech so that your own language penetrates. There need be nothing inauthentic in a way of speaking that is considered, graceful and poignant or dramatic.

- Make frequent use of writing activities for your student's own benefit. Writing is an excellent form of creative silence, of giving time for thought.

- Use variety to create a constant balance between absorption in the work (reverie), concentration on the work (effort), and recovery from the work (moving on to other things).

- Use your intuition and your own mood and energy level to guide your pacing and choice of activities. If you are bored or strained, the chances are your student will be too.

- Do not feel that you need to fill every minute. Allow spaces in time. Feel free to 'get up and move around' and your students will allow themselves to relax too.

Here is an alternative summary, looking at different kinds of 'Space'.

Desk space	Keeping desk or table free of clutter and awesome textbooks. Adopting a 'minimalist' strategy, using minimal aids and equipment, for example the Walkman recorder.
Space for movement	Encouraging and allowing yourself and the student freedom of movement. Not being glued to a chair or to any one position. Space for movement is space for relaxation.
Sensory space	Not putting up with spartan or drab cells. Respecting needs for sensory stimuli and providing a positive suggestive environment for learning.
Communicative space	Responding rather than reacting to the student. Making full use of silence, pausing and gesture. Keeping to a natural communicative rhythm of address and response, give and take, push and pull.
Space for student in-put	Providing formats through which students can present and re-present themselves, their companies, jobs and products. Making 'needs-analysis' a format for student presentations. Using the Cuisenaire format.
Mental and emotional space	Keeping planning skeletal. Leaving space in your mind to focus on the student. Knowing which feelings you regard as 'improper' in one-to-one.
Space for listening	Using and teaching 'auditing' skills: auditing pronunciation features, transcripts, signals and discourse moves. Feeding back your own awareness of your student's signals and discourse. Encouraging 'passive' listening.
Student - learning space	Thinking in terms of degrees of learner independence rather than 'level'. Discussing and negotiating the options at each stage. Allowing the student time to work alone, and being prepared to leave the room.
Imaginative space	Letting the non-verbal imagery (including recollected and anticipated situations) evoked by any activity be your guide to its value. Using techniques such as eliciting imagery, and projective identification.
Space for recollection	Using the time immediately after a lesson to inwardly recollect and review your interaction with the student—on the unspoken as well as the spoken level.

Auditing tapes

The purpose of these activities is to help the student observe spoken text more carefully.

Listening visualisation

- Listen and form a picture of the place
  eg a hotel: remember the last time you were in a hotel.
  What did it look like inside?
- Listen and form a picture of the speakers (from the tone of voice)
  eg sex, age, appearance, height, dress, gestures

Listening identification

- Listen and imagine you are there: where are you sitting/standing, what can you see? what are you doing there?
- Listen and identify with one of the speakers: where are you sitting/standing? how are you feeling? what gestures do you make? who are you facing and what expression are you making?

Listening anticipation, recollection, and response

Teacher stops tape at various points or uses a paused or open dialogue:

- Listen and repeat the speaker's last words
- Listen and anticipate the speaker's next words
- Listen and respond to the speaker

These are good ways of auditing complete as well as open dialogues.

Mental recollection, anticipation, and response

- Listen and imagine yourself responding in the pauses
- Listen and visualize a speaker responding in the pauses
- Listen and hear a speaker responding in the pauses

What does (s)he say? How does (s)he say it? How is (s)he sitting, standing, feeling, looking? What gestures/expressions does the speaker have?

- Listen again and see if you want to change your picture.
- Listen again and identify with another speaker.
- Listen, identify with a speaker and anticipate the next speaker's response.
- Listen and imagine an alternative response.

Auditing texts

These activities help the student observe written text more carefully.

Scanning

- Find a word or phrase which means ......
- Find a word or phrase used to request/suggest/offer something
- Find a word or phrase through which the speaker confirms that (s)he is listening
- Underline all verbs referring to past time

Gap-filling

- Fill in the missing words
- Fill in the missing preposition
- Fill in the verbs in the correct form

Correction

- Cross out all the unnecessary words
- Correct the errors

Jigsaw reconstruction

- Arrange the extracts/turns/sentences in their correct order
- Number the extracts/turns/sentences in their correct order

Information gap

- Find out from me what you need to know to complete the text/table sentences/article

Information transfer

- Transfer the information from text to chart or vice versa
- Write a summary/letter/report based on the information in the text
- Reorganise the information under the following headings

Comprehension

- True/False discrimination of statements
- Multiple choice identification of meaning
- Identification of missing information
- Judgement, evaluation and decision-making based on text

Reading aloud

- Correcting errors or filling gaps
- With emphasis on speech work for addressing an audience
- In a different tense/person

Comparing

- Two or more examples of the same type of text (eg adverts)
- The same text presented in different registers

Visualisation

- Reading dialogue and forming a picture of the situation and speakers

Guessing

- Reading and guessing the meaning of words from context
- Reading and substituting appropriate words for others not understood
- Reading and guessing the meaning of nonsense words from context

Listing

- Items of vocabulary, conjunctions, prepositions
- References to the past or future

Sorting lists

- Sorting references to past time into *(have)* plus participle and simple past forms
- Sorting into nouns, verbs, adjectives etc